The Five Good Emperors: The History of the Roman 1 Reigns of Nerva, Trajan, Hadrian, Antoninus Pius, an

By Charles River Editors

An ancient bust of Trajan

About Charles River Editors

Charles River Editors provides superior editing and original writing services across the digital publishing industry, with the expertise to create digital content for publishers across a vast range of subject matter. In addition to providing original digital content for third party publishers, we also republish civilization's greatest literary works, bringing them to new generations of readers via ebooks.

Sign up here to receive updates about free books as we publish them, and visit Our Kindle Author Page to browse today's free promotions and our most recently published Kindle titles.

Introduction

The Five Good Emperors

An ancient statue of Nerva

"From the study of this history we may also learn how a good government is to be established; for while all the emperors who succeeded to the throne by birth, except Titus, were bad, all were good who succeeded by adoption, as in the case of the five from Nerva to Marcus. But as soon as the empire fell once more to the heirs by birth, its ruin recommenced…Titus, Nerva, Trajan, Hadrian, Antoninus, and Marcus had no need of praetorian cohorts, or of countless legions to guard them, but were defended by their own good lives, the good-will of their subjects, and the attachment of the senate." – Niccolo Machiavelli

"If a man were called upon to fix that period in the history of the world during which the condition of the human race was most happy and prosperous he would, without hesitation, name that which elapsed from the deaths of Domitian to the accession of Commodus."[1] – Edward

---

[1] Chapter 3, p. 93, *The History of the Decline and Fall of the Roman Empire, Vol. 1* by E. Gibbon (H. Trevor-Roper,

Gibbon

"The Five Good Emperors," a reference to the five emperors who ruled the Roman Empire between 96 and 180 CE (Nerva, Trajan, Hadrian, Antoninus Pius, and Marcus Aurelius), was a term first coined by Machiavelli[2] and later adopted and popularized by historian Edward Gibbon, who said that under these men, the Roman Empire "was governed by absolute power under the guidance of wisdom and virtue."[3]

This period of 84 years is generally regarded as the high point of the Roman Empire, at least after Augustus, but what is uncertain and a matter of ongoing debate is whether the five emperors were personally responsible for the situation and the accompanying prosperity enjoyed throughout the empire at the time or if they were simply the beneficiaries of the *Pax Romana*, inaugurated by Augustus in the early part of the 1st century CE. In other words, historians have wondered whether anyone in power during those years would have enjoyed the same rewards.

The description of these rulers as "good" is also a matter of interpretation, with some scholars suggesting they were only "good" in comparison to the preceding emperor (Domitian) and the emperor who followed Marcus Aurelius (Commodus). Both of them were horrible rulers in every aspect, making their near contemporaries look all the better.

Regardless, it is clear that the era of the Five Good Emperors was one of unparalleled success and wealth, and the reasons Rome reached its zenith at this time are worthy of scrutiny. Perhaps most noteworthy is that none of these five emperors were blood relatives - while the final two are often referred to as the Antonines, they were not, in fact, related except by adoption, a practice that may in itself provide at least part of the answer to the question as to why this particular period was so magnificent.

These 84 years also witnessed an impressive growth in the size of the Roman Empire. New acquisitions ranged from northern Britain to Arabia, Mesopotamia, and Dacia. Furthermore, existing possessions were consolidated, and the empire's defenses improved when compared to what had come before. A range of countries that had been client states became fully integrated provinces, and even Italy saw administrative reforms which created further wealth. Throughout the empire, the policy of Romanization proved successful, at least in terms of introducing a common language, enabling standards of living to rise, and creating a political system minimizing internal strife.

With all of that said, according to some academics, the success these rulers had in centralizing the empire's administration, while undoubtedly bringing huge benefits, also sowed the seeds for

ed., 6 volumes 1993-1994). New York: Everyman's Library.

[2] Machiavelli *Discourses on Livy*, I. 10.4.

[3] *The History of the Decline and Fall of the Roman Empire* by E. Gibbon (H. Trevor-Roper, ed., 6 volumes 1993-1994). New York: Everyman's Library.

later problems. After all, as so many Roman emperors proved, from Caligula and Nero to Commodus, the empire's approach to governance was predicated on the ruler's ability. When incompetent or insane emperors came to power, the whole edifice came tumbling down.

The Five Good Emperors: The History of the Roman Empire during the Reigns of Nerva, Trajan, Hadrian, Antoninus Pius, and Marcus Aurelius looks at these emperors' lives and reigns, and how Rome flourished during that time. Along with pictures depicting important people, places, and events, you will learn about the Five Good Emperors like never before.

The Five Good Emperors: The History of the Roman Empire during the Reigns of Nerva, Trajan, Hadrian, Antoninus Pius, and Marcus Aurelius

Nerva

The imperial process of Rome began with the assassination of Julius Caesar, and the rise to power on November 26, 43 BCE, of a triumvirate of powerful men, Gaius Octavius (Octavian, Caesar Augustus), Marcus Antonius (Mark Antony), and Marcus Aemilius Lepidus. This three-pointed leadership came into being with the enactment of the Lex Titia, a powerful Roman law that passed on November 27, 43 BCE, and which legalized the Second Triumvirate, granting the three men engaged within it the authority to act as a "…three-man commission for restoring the constitution of the republic." This insulated these individuals from censure or any level of oversight or control by the senate, which marked the effective twilight of the Roman Republic and the dawn of the Roman Empire.

Although the republic was divided into three portions, each ruled by one member of the Triumvirate, it was inevitable that this uneasy balance of power and authority would not in the end be able to survive against the individual ambitions of each member. Ultimately, Marcus Aemilius Lepidus was driven into exile and stripped of his position, and Mark Antony committed suicide following his defeat at the Battle of Actium by Octavian in 31 BC. This left Augustus in a position to consolidate the disparate factions of the republic, and thereafter consolidate it into the Roman Empire.

History remembers the 40-year reign of Augustus as a period of peace, imperial expansion and prosperity. The outer regions and provinces of the empire were pacified and stabilized, aided by the professionalization of the army and the advance of a vast network of land communications. The reign of Augustus was followed by that of his adopted son and heir Tiberius, who in general followed the precepts laid down by his predecessor, maintaining the professionalism of the army and the outer boundaries of the empire, while at the same time pursuing conservative fiscal policies that enriched both his own and the coffers of the exchequer considerably. Tiberius, however, according at least to the historian Tacitus, was a morally corrupt and cruel individual, who, for all of his attributes, followed a Machiavellian philosophy of power and authority, which in due course he passed on to his nephew and heir, the infamous Caligula.

Caligula almost personifies the popular image of a debauched and insane emperor, drunk on power and unrestrained by any limitations on personal behavior and power. To a degree this was true, and certainly the short reign of Caligula offered numerous examples of excess and borderline insanity.

A period of relative restraint and prosperity followed Caligula's assassination in 41 CE (after only four years on the throne), and the succession of his uncle, Emperor Claudius, but ultimately, it was Claudius's successor Nero who oversaw the end of the line. The steadily mounting corruption and compromise of Roman leadership reached its crescendo, and the list of Nero's iniquities, real or imagined, is long.

In 54 CE, at the age of 16, he ascended to the imperial throne, and for the most part his arrival was well received. Among his early achievements was the granting of certain basic rights to slaves, the strengthening of the senate, a reduction in taxes and the general encouragement of modesty and restraint. He was initially attentive to the military, the central pillar of imperial power, and indeed, it was during his reign that the British resistance was broken in the aftermath of the rebellion of the Iceni Queen Boadicea, which in 61 CE resulted in a signature Roman victory.

However, with the passage of time, the darker side of Nero's nature gradually began to manifest, and his cruelty and instability began to erode his early popularity. On July 18, 64 CE, Rome burned, with 3 of its 14 precincts destroyed and 7 others critically damaged. Although Nero responded to the disaster responsibly, by providing what assistance he could to those affected, rumors nonetheless circulated that he had been responsible for the fire, or at the very least had stood by and allowed it to consume those parts of Rome that he desired for the grandiose public works and building projects with which he was credited. In response to this, he blamed Christians for the fire, beginning the signature persecution of Roman Christians that has been so widely recorded in Roman history. Nero was eventually declared a public enemy, and finding himself without support, he committed suicide on June 9, 68 CE, the first Roman emperor to do so.

Having left no heir, Nero's death plunged the empire into confusion and chaos, bringing to an end the Julio-Claudian lineage while at the same time offering no clear rule of succession. This presented the opportunity for influential individuals in the empire, and in particular provincial governors who also commanded large military garrisons, to express and further their own ambitions to power. The result was a period of instability and civil war as several pretenders to the throne, among them the emperors Galba, Otho and Vitellius, gained and lost power, until finally the emperor Vespasian seized and retained the imperial principate. Vespasian imposed order and discipline on a chaotic empire and founded the Flavian Dynasty, which survived until 96, encompassing the reigns of Vespasian himself (69–79) and his two sons, Titus (79–81) and Domitian (81–96).

José Luiz Bernardes Ribeiro's picture of an ancient bust of Domitian

In the midst of all that turmoil, future emperors were born and rising through the ranks. Marcus Cocceius Nerva was born in 35 CE in Narnia, approximately 35 miles north of Rome. His father was a wealthy lawyer, and a number of his family members had held office within the Roman system. His great-grandfather had been a consul in 36 BCE, and at the time of his birth, his family was still very much part of court circles.

Nerva was linked with the Julio-Claudians on his mother's side, and his aunt was Tiberius' great-granddaughter. Like his grandfather and father, Nerva followed the fairly standard route for young Romans. In 65 CE, he helped suppress the conspiracy against Nero led by Piso, and despite his association with that reviled emperor, he was made a co-consul by Vespasian in 71 CE. Similarly, Emperor Domitian chose him as his co-consul in 90 CE.

While his ability to steer a course through what were undoubtedly turbulent waters is testimony to his political acumen, there can be no doubt his success was, in part, due to the esteem in which Romans of his class held him. This respect was most evident on 18 September, 96 CE, the day Domitian was murdered. The *Fasti Ostienses* recorded Nerva's elevation to the throne by the Senate in a singularly terse inscription: "Fourteenth day before the Kalends of October Domitian killed. On the same day Marcus Ciocceius Nerva proclaimed Emperor."[4] This was the first occasion on which the Senate had elected an emperor.

It is quite clear that Nerva did not seek power prior to the death of Domitian, but rather had it thrust upon him. Cassius Dio claimed the conspirators approached Nerva before carrying out the assassination, and in fear of his life, he felt he had no option but to go along with their plans.[5] Whether Cassius Dio's claims are true or not, what is known is that the Senate welcomed his accession with enthusiasm. Dio records that in the following months, there was an outpouring of hatred for Domitian, and statues, arches, and other structures associated with him were destroyed. Many close to him were murdered or exiled, and those he had exiled were allowed to return to Rome.

During this period, there was a sense of both relief and euphoria. Cassius Dio remarked that under Domitian, no one could do anything at all, but under Nerva, they could do whatever they pleased. This situation rapidly descended into a kind of free-for-all, and the 60-year-old emperor, old by the standards of the day, seemed unable to regain the same type of control Domitian had before him. Nerva is said to have been quite ill when he came to power, and the deteriorating situation did little to aid his digestive problems.

Despite these initial obstacles, however, he managed to establish himself as emperor, calling Gibbon's ultimately unflattering assessment of him into question: "[Nerva] had scarcely accepted the purple from the assassins of Domitian before he discovered that his feeble age was unable to stem the torrent of public disorders which had multiplied under the long tyranny of his predecessor. His mild disposition was respected by the good but the degenerate Romans required a more vigorous character whose justice should strike terror into the guilty."[6]

Gibbon's criticisms aside, Nerva quickly came to be seen as a benevolent ruler. He won people over by allocating land to the urban poor, confirming that he would never execute Roman Senators, embarking on a program of public works that included repairs to existing roads and aqueducts, providing employment, and improving the standard of living for many ordinary Romans.

---

[4] P. 153, 'M. Cocceius Nerva and the Flavians' *by C.L. Murison (2003). Transactions of the American Philological Association.* **133** *(1): 147–157.*

[5] Cassius Dio, *Roman History*, LI.

[6] *The History of the Decline and Fall of the Roman Empire, Vol. 1* by E. Gibbon (H. Trevor-Roper, ed., 6 volumes 1993-1994). New York: Everyman's Library.

These measures made him extremely popular in many quarters, but he did not win over the army. While he had alienated just about everyone else, Domitian had kept the army on board by giving them regular pay raises, but Nerva did not follow suit, and military dissatisfaction came to a head in 97 CE, when the Praetorian Guard staged a mutiny. Nerva was imprisoned by Casperius Aelianus, the Praetorian commander, who demanded that Petronius and Parthenius - leaders of the conspiracy against Domitian - be surrendered to him. It is said that Nerva refused the demand, going as far as bearing his own throat to the mutineers rather than hand over their assassins. Eventually, the two conspirators were brutally murdered. Nerva's authority was severely damaged by the affair, but he suffered no personal injury, and Trajan ultimately went on to mete out justice to the rebellious Praetorian commander.

In previous situations where an emperor had lost the confidence of the military, it was typical for him to be replaced relatively quickly. Nerva was old and childless, and it did not seem likely that he would last very long at all. However, he did something that secured his position and provided the blueprint for successors who would face similar dilemmas in later years by adopting someone. Through this method, he took Marcus Ulpius Traianus - more commonly known to the world as Trajan - as his heir.

Whether the adoption of Trajan was a brilliant scheme devised by Nerva or something forced upon him by the army is an open question. What is not in doubt is the fact that this action was what allowed him to live out the remainder of his life in peace and tranquility. A few months before his death, he reportedly said, "I have done nothing as Emperor that would prevent me laying down the imperial office and returning to private life in safety."[7]

When Nerva became emperor, he was awarded the title of *Pater Patriae* ("Father of his Country"), an honor previously awarded to emperors well into their reigns, and this admiration continued after his death. His short 16-month reign ended with his death from natural causes in January 98 CE, after which the Senate deified him. It is a mark of the inordinate degree of respect in which he was held that his ashes were interred in the Mausoleum of Augustus alongside those of the Julio-Claudians. Nerva was a popular emperor with the Senate, an achievement in itself, and there is no reason to doubt that he was as kind and generous-hearted a man as believed. Apart from the uncorroborated claim that he sexually abused Domitian as a boy, there are still questions as to how, precisely, he managed to maintain various positions under two of the most ruthless and tyrannical emperors Rome had ever witnessed before his accession to becoming emperor.

While acknowledging the effectiveness of his program of public works, remission of taxes, and reforms which benefitted the people, more cynical people speculate as to whether these policies were more akin to bribery than an enlightened approach to governance. Nonetheless, it's indisputable that by choosing Trajan as his successor, he deserved the gratitude showered upon

---

[7] Cassius Dio, *Roman* History, LXVIII.

him. Pliny summed the situation up succinctly when he wrote, "There is no more certain proof of divinity in a ruler who has chosen his successor than the worthiness of his choice."[8] It can even be argued that Nerva's greatest achievement was ensuring the peaceful transition of power and ushering in Trajan's reign. Tacitus spoke of his reign in glowing terms, calling it "the dawn of a most happy age when Nerva blended things once irreconcilable, sovereignty and freedom."[9]

Trajan

Hartmann Linge's picture of a statue of Trajan in a military outfit

---

[8] Pliny, *Panegyricus (Letters)*, XI.
[9] Tacitus, *Agricola*, 3.

Trajan has long been considered one of the greatest and best-known of all Roman emperors. During his 19-year reign, the boundaries of the Roman Empire were pushed to their greatest extent, and in addition to his military achievements, he also developed the administration of the government so successfully that his relationships with the Senate and the people were extraordinarily positive. Cassius Dio would write of him, "His association with the people was marked by affability and his intercourse with the Senate by dignity so that he was loved by all and dreaded by none save the enemy."[10]

Trajan was born in Italica near modern-day Seville in 53 CE, which meant he would be the first non-Italian emperor in Roman history. Though his family had roots in Umbria, they were far from being rustic or provincial. His father was Marcus Ulpius Traianus, commander of the Tenth Legion in the First Jewish War, who became a Consul in 70 CE. At the end of his term in office, Trajan's father was made governor of Syria, and in his lifetime he also served as governor of Baetica and Asia. He died sometime before 100 CE, with the exact date remaining unknown.

Given the backing of such a powerful family, it is of little surprise that Trajan was able to progress quickly through the positions necessary for able and ambitious Roman aristocrats. He served as Tribune under his father in Syria, and by the late 80s CE, he was commanding the Seventh Legion, stationed in northern Spain. In 89 CE, he took his legion to Germany to help Domitian suppress the rebellion against him—led by Saturninus. Though he arrived too late to take any military role, the emperor looked favorably on his support, rewarding his loyalty by making him a Consul in 91 CE

Though Domitian was unpopular, Trajan's association with him did not hinder his career, and in 96 CE, when Nerva became emperor, he was made governor of Upper Germany. It was while he was serving there in 97 CE that Trajan received a letter from the emperor telling him that he had adopted him. The practice of an emperor adopting an heir was instituted by Augustus when he adopted Tiberius as his son. It is not known whether Trajan knew of Nerva's intention in advance, though there has always been the suspicion that the adoption was engineered by Trajan's friends in Rome, who may have put pressure on the elderly emperor. There have also been suggestions that Trajan actively prompted his supporters to work on Nerva to secure his adoption.

In the end, the move proved highly successful for all concerned. Trajan intervened in the mutiny instigated by Casperius Aelianus by sending for the ringleaders and executing them when they arrived. He thereby ensured that Nerva would not be troubled by threats from the military for the remainder of his reign.

When Nerva died in 98 CE, Trajan felt so secure in his position as emperor that he did not immediately return to Rome. Instead, he embarked on a tour of the Rhine garrisons and Danube

---

[10] Cassius Dio, *Roman History*, LXVIII.

frontier. This visit had more than a military purpose as the Danube frontier was where a third of the Roman army was stationed at the time. His visit helped secure the loyalty of troops who had worshipped Domitian, enabling him to become, in their minds, Domitian's real successor.

The new emperor did not arrive in Rome until the summer of 99 CE, during which throngs of enthusiastic citizens greeted him. Trajan knew how to win a crowd, and he entered Rome on foot and mingled with the people, embracing every Senator in turn. This projection of personal modesty and humility would become the hallmark of his public persona in the years to come. In reality, however, he retained all Imperial power garnered by previous emperors and remained an absolute monarch, though he also conducted his affairs with the Senators in a dignified and restrained manner, an approach in marked contrast to that of Domitian.

The substance of autocratic rule remained intact, and it was he who chose the Consuls and all the other important officials governing the empire. His tactics worked, and his success in managing his class can be found in the words of Pliny the Younger in September 100 CE when he took up his position as Consul. Pliny's published description of the emperor's virtues took six hours to read aloud. This written version is sycophantic to the extreme and contains lavish praise extolling Trajan's abilities, his virtues, and his piety. In one section, Pliny praiseed Trajan's preferred mode of relaxation, the hunt, where he claimed the emperor liked to "range the forests, drive wild beasts from their lairs, scale vast mountain heights, and set foot on rocky crags with none to give a helping hand or show the way amidst all of this to visit the sacred groves in a spirit of devotion and present himself to deities there."[11] Pliny also praised Trajan's wife, Plotina, in his panegyric: "How modest she is in her attire, how moderate in the number of her attendants, how unassuming when she walks abroad."[12]

There is no doubt that Pliny was somewhat over the top in his description of the emperor, but there is ample other evidence to suggest that Trajan was a very able ruler. Writing some years after the emperor's death, Galen praised his program of building and repairing roads, especially his insistence on paving muddy sections, as being of particular practical benefit. He also mentioned Trajan's bridge-building and numerous other engineering projects, all of which are confirmed by inscriptions dotted throughout the empire that describe the work undertaken.

Perhaps one of the most unusual steps taken by Trajan, one that added to his popularity and reputation, was his scheme to help the poor and children in particular. He set imperial funds, known as *alimenta*, aside to provide for their upkeep. The policy lasted for nearly 200 years.

Roman contemporaries praised Trajan's piety, but he was no religious zealot, as made clear in his response to a request from Pliny, then governor of Bythinia, for advice on how to deal with Christians. Unsure about how to deal with those accused of being practicing Christians by

[11] Pliny, *Panegyricus (Letters)*, X.
[12] Pliny, *Panegyricus (Letters)*, X.

anonymous informants, Trajan's response demonstrates that he was a man of acumen and sensitivity: "You have followed the course of action which you should in investigating the cases of those brought before you accused of being Christians, for it is not possible to establish a fixed rule which would apply to all cases. These people must not be sought out, if they are brought before you and the charge is proved, they must be punished but any of them who denies he is a Christian and gives visible evidence of that by praying to our Gods, however much he may have been previously suspected, let him be given a pardon for his penitence. The anonymous pamphlets which have been published must have no place in any accusation. For on the one hand they give a very bad example and on the other they are not the way things should now be done."[13]

Of course, Trajan was not perfect, and some Romans took note of his personal vices. Cassius Dio claimed that Trajan was too fond of boys and wine, and that Trajan took too much pleasure in war, though he was careful to excuse his emperor's love of military adventure: "And even if he did delight in war, nevertheless he was satisfied when success had been achieved, a most bitter foe overthrown and his countrymen exalted."[14]

Trajan's military successes account for the way his contemporaries and history hold him in high esteem. He excelled in the art of war, and his bravery and willingness to share in the trials and tribulations of his troops endeared him to them. It is only fair to point out that when he became emperor, Rome did not face any serious external threat, so it is not unreasonable to conclude that his campaigns resulted from his predilection for military projects. It is also true that such a large army had to be kept busy, a fact that would, no doubt, have also played its part in his decisions to engage in military action.

Trajan initiated three major campaigns during his reign, the first of which was against the Dacians. Dacia was a kingdom north of the Danube frontier in what is now modern Roumania. The pretext for the war was Trajan's claim that Dacian King Decebalus had broken the terms of the peace negotiated by Domitian between Rome and Dacia. Whether there was any real justification for the expedition in terms of security is unclear, but Trajan invaded Dacia in 101 CE, winning a major victory near Tapae. The campaign ended the following year with a Dacian defeat, and the empire gained large swathes of land. Trajan returned to Rome and was awarded a triumph, as well the title *Dacicus* by the Senate.

The peace did not last long, so in 105 CE, Trajan once more led Roman legions into Dacia, aided by the new bridge he had built across the Danube. Cassius Dio asserted that the construction of this bridge surpassed anything else the emperor achieved, writing, "Brilliant indeed as are his other achievements yet this surpasses them."[15]

Though Trajan had been relatively lenient in the terms for peace he imposed on Dacia in the

---

[13] Pliny, *Panegyricus (Letters)*, X. 97.
[14] Cassius Dio, *Roman History*, LXI.
[15] Cassius Dio, *Roman History*, LXVIII. 13.

previous war, he was utterly ruthless on this occasion. Sarmizegetusa, the capital city, was razed to the ground, and Dacian King Decebalus was mercilessly hounded until he committed suicide. The emperor was not content even then, as he had his enemy's head cut off and mounted on the steps of the Capitol. Trajan ransacked the country, carting off any treasures he could find, and his tactics resulted in the successful crushing of Dacia and its integration into the empire as a province.

The campaign is commemorated in the carvings around Trajan's column set up by the Senate in the Forum in Rome. The column provides invaluable information about Roman military equipment and details when it comes to how Roman troops dressed and fought, but what is more significant is how it emphasizes the personal contribution Trajan made to the victory. The column depicts Trajan receiving reports and missions from foreign embassies and sacrificing and accepting the surrender of the defeated Dacians. He is portrayed as a commanding figure worthy of respect in all depictions.

A picture of the ruins of Trajan's Forum and Trajan's Column

A depiction of the Romans fighting the Dacians from Trajan's Column

Trajan's victorious return was the excuse for yet another triumph and a whole series of some of the most elaborate spectacles ever seen in Rome. Events included public games in which 10,000 gladiators took part, a similar number of wild animals were killed, and huge amounts of food were provided for the masses. He used the enormous booty he had accumulated to fund these extravagances, but he also used part of the plunder to finance a new harbor at Ostia, add embellishments to the Forum, and begin construction of a new market and a completely new Forum. The Forum of Trajan was officially opened at the beginning of 112 CE, and Trajan's Column was placed there the following year.

These projects were completed from 107-113, a time of peace and plenty when Trajan concentrated on projects other than war. Pliny the Younger, in his *Panegyric,* was impressed by Trajan's ambition in relation to these projects: "But when it comes to public building, you do it on a grand scale. Here stands a colonnade, there a shrine, rising as if by magic, so rapidly as to seem remodelled rather than freshly built. Elsewhere the vast façade of the Circus rivals the beauty of the temples, a fitting place for a nation which has conquered the world."[16]

In addition to the buildings already mentioned, Trajan used the wealth won in Dacia to build the Baths of Trajan on the site of Nero's Golden House, the Naumachia Traiani (an amphitheater built to stage mock sea battles), and the Aqua Traiana, the last of the great aqueducts built to bring water into the city. Outside of Rome, Trajan was equally active, ; apart from the harbor at Ostia, he funded new colonies for veterans, including Timgad in North Africa, Sarmizegetusa in

---

[16] Pliny in his Panegyric (51)

Dacia, and Nijmegen and Xanten in the Rhineland. Centuries later, Constantine the Great referred to him unflatteringly as a wall-growing creeper due to the number of buildings bearing inscriptions to or about him in the empire.

Trajan returned to the campaign trail in 114 CE, and he would spend the rest of his life fighting on the eastern frontier. On this occasion, the enemy was the Parthians, against which Roman armies had a very poor record. The tentative peace between the two old adversaries was shattered when the Parthians placed their candidate on the throne of Armenia, a buffer state separating the two greater powers. Trajan acted decisively, marched into Armenia, and made it a Roman province.

In what is regarded as a truly brilliant military campaign the following year, he marched into Mesopotamia and captured the Parthian capital of Ctesiphon near modern-day Baghdad. According to Cassius Dio, Trajan relied on engineering technology more than military might to conquer Ctesiphon: "Trajan had planned to conduct the Euphrates through a canal into the Tigris, in order that he might take his boats down by this route and use them to make a bridge. But learning that this river has a much higher elevation than the Tigris, he did not do so, fearing that the water might rush down in a flood and render the Euphrates unnavigable. So he used hauling-engines to drag the boats across the very narrow space that separates the two rivers (the whole stream of the Euphrates empties into a marsh and from there somehow joins the Tigris); then he crossed the Tigris and entered Ctesiphon. When he had taken possession of this place he was saluted imperator and established his right to the title of Parthicus. In addition to other honours voted to him by the senate, he was granted the privilege of celebrating as many triumphs as he should desire." (Cassius Dio, *Roman History*, LXVIII, 28, 1-3).

These successes gave the Romans an outlet into the Persian Gulf, but that success was short-lived and rebellions in 116 CE, followed by his failure to take the city of Hatra the following year, took the gloss from his campaign. Although Trajan was given triumphs and columns were erected that proclaimed his victories in the Near East over the Parthians, the Romans were unable to hold onto Ctesiphon. In fact, the Parthian city would continue to be the focal point of conflict between the Romans and Parthians for so long that the Roman general Avidius Cassius would lead a major campaign against Seleucia and Ctesiphon during the reign of Marcus Aurelius a few generations later.

As Trajan tried to fight the Parthians, he had to deal with a number of other crises, especially when it came to the Jews. The conflict known as the Kitos War was fought between 115 and 117, and it is sometimes called the rebellion of the diaspora because it involved Jewish communities scattered throughout the Roman world. In 115, Trajan was commanding an expedition against the Parthians, but while he advanced without any real opposition through Mesopotamia, Jewish rebels took the opportunity to attack the small Roman garrisons that Trajan left behind as he marched eastwards. Other Jewish revolts in Cyprus, Cyrenaica, and Egypt encouraged the rebels in Judea, and cities with large Jewish populations such as Nisibis, Edessa, Seleucia, and Arbela took advantage of Trajan's preoccupation with the Parthians. Roman garrisons were slaughtered throughout the territories in the rebellion.

In Cyrenaica, the rebels were led by Andreas and destroyed anything that was connected to Rome, including temples and public buildings such as baths and the Caesareum. Orosius claimed that rebel savagery so depopulated the region that it had to be resettled much later by Hadrian: "The Jews waged war on the inhabitants throughout Libya in the most savage fashion, and to such an extent was the country wasted that its cultivators having been slain, its land would have remained utterly depopulated had not the Emperor Hadrian gathered settlers from other places and sent them thither, for the inhabitants had been wiped out."[17]

Cassius Dio wrote of these revolts, "Meanwhile the Jews in the region of Cyrene had put one Andreas at their head and were destroying both the Romans and the Greeks. They would cook their flesh, make belts for themselves of their entrails, anoint themselves with their blood and wear their skins for clothing. Many they sawed in two from the head downwards. Others they would give to wild beasts and force still others to fight as gladiators. In all, consequently, two hundred and twenty thousand perished. In Egypt also they performed many similar deeds and in Cyprus under the leadership of Aertemion. There likewise two hundred and forty thousand perished. For this reason no Jew may set foot in that land, but even if one of them is driven upon the island by force of wind he is put to death. Various persons took part in subduing these Jews one being Lusius who was sent by Trajan."[18]

There is probably some truth in the claims that Cassius Dio's account was exaggerated, but there is little doubt that the Jewish rebels, exasperated by years of repression and encouraged by hopes of freedom from Rome, acted as savagely to the Romans as the Romans had to them in previous years.

In Egypt, Jews set fire to Alexandria and destroyed temples. They remained on the rampage until they were eventually defeated in 117 by Marcius Turbo. Similarly, the revolt in Cyprus was put down with great savagery, resulting in all Jews being expelled from the island. While these revolts were playing out, a further revolt sprang up in Mesopotamia, and Trajan, realizing the danger of the situation, took steps to deal with the Parthian problem by giving them a king from among their own nobility so he could turn his attention to the insurrection.

Trajan undertook a siege of Hatra, but he died suddenly at Traianopolis on August 9, 117 after suffering a stroke or heatstroke. His body was returned to Rome and his ashes placed at the foot of his column. The whole empire mourned him, and in later years, the Senate prayed that new emperors be "More fortunate than Augustus and better than Trajan."

---

[17] Orosius, *Seven Books of History Against the Pagans*, 7.12.6.
[18] Cassius Dio, *Roman History*, V. 68 32.

Trajan set the standard by which future emperors were judged, and his reputation lasted so long that during the Middle Ages, Dante gave him a place in Heaven, something that was not done for other pre-Christian Emperors.

Hadrian

An ancient bust of Hadrian

Trajan's successor was his adopted son, Hadrian, who would prove to be as effective as his predecessor. Aurelius Victor, in his *Book of the Caesars,* summed up the character and personality of the emperor who has become one of the most respected of all of Rome's rulers: "Aelius Hadrianus was more suited to eloquence and the studies of peacetime and after peace had been restored in the east he returned to Rome. There he began to devote his attention to religious rituals, to laws, to the gymnasia and to teachers so that he established an institute of liberal arts which was called the Athenaeum."[19]

If so, the new emperor, in contrast to his predecessor, was a man of culture and the arts rather than war. Further evidence confirms that Hadrian did not take joy in his military campaigns, and whenever he could, he preferred avoiding military action. The preference for peaceful solutions has resulted in history judging him as a pragmatic, ruler. He concentrated his energy on improving the internal structures of the empire and following policies that provided the empire with 20 years of sound, stable government.

Publius Aelius Hadrianus was born in 76, but there is a dispute as to whether his birthplace was Rome or Italica. Although Roman in origin, his family had settled in Italica 300 years prior. His family was well-connected, and Hadrian's father was a cousin of Trajan. In 86 CE, when his father died, he became a ward of Trajan and a Roman knight named Acilius Attianus.

There are various tales told of Hadrian's wild youth, including a story that claimed Trajan tried to set him off on his political career when he was only 15 years old but gave up due to his obsession with hunting (somewhat at odds with his later indifference to military action). Hadrian's love of the good life resulted in Trajan's bringing him to Rome, where he could keep a tighter leash on the boy. Despite his youth, Trajan made Hadrian a judge in one of the courts dealing with disputes over inheritance. This was followed by appointments to the Second and Fifth Legions, both of which served on the Danube.

In 97 CE, when Trajan, then on the Rhine, was adopted by Nerva, it was Hadrian who was chosen to go to Trajan to convey the congratulations of the troops. It is said that his determination to be among the first to reach the new heir resulted in him traveling a great deal of the way on foot. His enthusiasm seems to have paid dividends when a close friendship developed between the two men. Hadrian soon rose to the position of commander of a legion. After Rome's victory in the east he was made a Praetor, Governor of Lower Pannonia, and Consul in successive years between 106 and 108 CE.

During Trajan's Parthian Campaign, Hadrian served as Governor of Syria, but despite the favor with which Trajan treated him, there was no indication he intended to name Hadrian as his successor. In fact, his position among the Roman elite was not considered particularly strong.

The whole matter of how Hadrian succeeded Trajan is somewhat of a mystery. Trajan's wife, Plotina, claimed the emperor had adopted Hadrian and named him as his successor while on his deathbed, but there is no corroborating evidence confirming her statement. Cassius Dio certainly did not believe Trajan's wife, and he went so far as to suggest she had hidden the fact of his death for a number of days so she could send a letter to the Senate telling them of Trajan's "decision" to adopt Hadrian. She excused the fact that the confirmation had been signed by her

---

[19] Aurelius Victor, *Book of the Caesars,* XIV.

rather than the emperor on the grounds that he was too weak. Another tale spread at the time was that Plotina had paid an actor to impersonate the emperor and announce the adoption, only revealing the emperor's death once convinced the succession was assured.

Hadrian was in Syria at the time of Trajan's death, and as soon as he was given the news, he traveled to Seleucia, where Trajan's body was. After the cremation ceremony, Hadrian took a rather circuitous route back to Rome to deal with a minor military matter on the Danube. His succession was relatively peaceful compared to that of many emperors, but unlike Trajan, his was tarnished by the deaths of four Senators, in what is known to history as "The Affair of the Four Senators." The four in question were all ex-consuls whom Hadrian's supporters claimed were plotting against Hadrian, but Cassius Dio put forward a different reason for their deaths: that Hadrian wanted to sequester their wealth. Hadrian never accepted responsibility for these deaths, and he swore an oath in public to that effect, claiming that the Senate had ordered the executions.[20] He then confirmed Nerva's pledge not to execute any Senators without the Senate's approval, but his protestations did little to convince many, and it is still the conclusion of most historians that he arranged for the deaths of men he considered potential rivals.

Having secured the throne, Hadrian focused his attention on ruling in a fashion he believed to be in Rome's best interests. He immediately abandoned territory won by Trajan in the east and returned to the policy initiated by Augustus of securing the empire in the lands that were, at the time, considered Rome's natural boundaries: the Rhine, the Danube, and the Euphrates. Hadrian was, undoubtedly, an energetic man who soon proved to be an efficient administrator with an eye for detail. He did not have Trajan's love of all things military, but he did focus his attention on making the army more effective and disciplined. He expanded the *alimenta* and was quickly accepted by the populace because of his obvious talents.

Hadrian had spent much of his career on the borders, and once he was emperor, he did not content himself to rule from his palace in Rome. In fact, he spent more than half his time outside of Italy, more than any other emperor, including visiting hotspots such as Gaul and far-flung regions such as Libya. Generally, he lived in army camps, dressing as a soldier and sharing their meals and sleeping quarters, but despite this martial air, Hadrian adopted a defensive strategy, abandoning Trajan's conquests in Mesopotamia because he thought they would be too difficult and costly to keep. Thus, in a sense, the reign of Trajan was the high-water mark of the Roman Empire from a territorial standpoint, and the policy from then on was more or less set by Hadrian: preserve the limits of the empire and only go beyond them to punish stubborn enemies.

It was in furtherance of these goals that Hadrian became one of the empire's great builders, with building fortifications on the border being one of his main goals. Hadrian strengthened fortifications along the Danube and Rhine, the two most troublesome borders, as well as other areas on the periphery of the empire. He also visited Britain, where he saw the need to protect the

---

[20] Historia Augusta, *Life of Hadrian*, X.

empire's northernmost border.

In 121, Hadrian traveled throughout Gaul, the Rhineland, and Britain. Following that, he visited Spain and Mauretania, and then sailed to Asia Minor and Greece. He only returned to Rome in 125 CE via the territories on the Danube. Three years later, he visited Tunisia. Later that same year, he visited Greece and Asia Minor, which took him to Syria, Judea, Egypt, and Libya before returning to Rome in 134 CE. These three major journeys took 10 years.

It was during this period that he visited northern England, "where he built a wall eighty miles long which separated the Romans and the barbarians."[21] Hadrian arrived at the province of Britannia in 122 to inspect it after the suppression of a fierce rebellion, probably by the Brigantes tribe aligned with tribes in the unoccupied north. It was suppressed by Governor Quintus Pompeius Falco, who had been assigned there by Trajan and continued his good work under Hadrian. Details are sketchy, but it appears to have been a bloody affair. Even two generations later, Marcus Cornelius Fronto wrote to the emperor Marcus Aurelius (ruled 161-180), "[W]hat a large number of soldiers were killed under your grandfather Hadrian by the Jews, what a number by the Britons."

Hadrian's decision to build a wall across the northern frontier was in keeping with his defensive strategy elsewhere. On the frontier with Germany, a much longer border, he built a timber palisade, but with the border to Caledonia being only 80 Roman miles, he deemed a stone wall possible. Other emperors had also fortified borders all around the empire. In North Africa, there were stretches of wall in sensitive areas, and though the border was far too long to fortify completely, regular blockhouses kept watch over most of it. In Raetia (modern Switzerland and Austria), there was a stone wall as well. None, however, were as ambitious and complex as the wall Hadrian envisioned.

During his visit, Hadrian declared a new goddess, Britannia, the female personification of the province, by striking coins in her honor. One of these coins showed Britannia in military clothing in a standard pose of the defeated, perhaps a celebration of the suppression of the revolt that happened late in Trajan's and early in Hadrian's reign. This wasn't the only official celebration of Hadrian's deeds. A fragmentary inscription that was used as building material for a church in Jarrow, a bit south of the River Tyne reads, "Son of all deified emperors, the Emperor Caesar Trajan Hadrian Augustus, after the necessity of keeping the empire within its limits that had been laid on him by divine command. . .once the barbarians had been scattered and the province of Britannia recovered, added a frontier between either shore of Ocean for 80 miles. The army of the province built the wall under the direction of Aulus Platorius Nepos, Pro-Praetorian Legate of Augustus."

Doubtless other inscriptions were made at the time, but an interesting aspect of this inscription

---

[21] *Historia Augusta*, Life of Hadrian, XI.

is the idea that the empire had divinely ordained limits. For much of its history, Rome's policy was one of constant expansion. Now Hadrian felt the empire had reached the largest size at which it could remain stable and wanted to consolidate and protect what he had. Considering the pressure from the German tribes and the Parthians, this was a wise move. The overcompensation of creating Hadrian's Wall for a frontier that, while troublesome, was never seriously going to threaten the empire's existence, showed that he wanted this frontier at least to be one that would never cause him worry. After he finished his visit to Britannia, Hadrian sailed to the province of Mauretania (part of modern Morocco) to suppress a revolt there. This long voyage was typical of the itinerant nature of the emperor.

A tremendous amount of timber was required to build the forts and other installations along Hadrian's Wall, as well as scaffolding and temporary shelters while the wall was under construction. Unlike today, in Roman times the borderlands between England and Scotland were heavily forested and timber was plentiful. Just clearing the land for the defensive system would have supplied a vast amount of wood.

An unusual feature of Hadrian's Wall, and one that has caused much discussion, is the Vallum, a flat-bottomed ditch 18-19.5 feet wide at the top, 7 feet wide at the bottom, and 9-10 feet deep. Low mounds on both the north and south sides measure 30-39.5 feet wide and 9-10 feet high. These were hardened with stacks of turf blocks.

Given the numerous uprisings among the Britons, the Vallum may have been to protect the wall's more vulnerable south side. This argument is weakened, however, by the fact that at times the Vallum lies far out of arrow range from the wall, at one point being a full mile away. Another purpose may have been to limit traffic, as the only places where cobblestone causeways are built across the Vallum are opposite the main forts. Other researchers have suggested it was a boundary marker delineating the transition from civilian to military space. All three of these theories may be correct.

There were originally 12 main forts along the length of Hadrian's Wall, although two more (Carrawburgh and Drumburgh) were added later. If forts near the wall are included, such as those at South Shields, Newcastle, and Carvoran, the total rises to 17. Spread roughly seven miles (11 km) apart, these were the main camps for the troops and controlled traffic between Caledonia and the Roman Empire. An estimated 10,000 troops garrisoned the wall and its forts.

There already was a line of forts along the Stanegate before Hadrian's Wall was constructed, but in places this road ran as much as two miles to the south of the wall. It was decided, despite the extra cost, to move the forts to the wall, but four Stanegate forts—Carvoran, Carlisle, Chesterholm, and Corbridge—were retained because of their proximity to the new line.

The main forts were laid out on a rectangular north-south plan and projected out beyond the wall to the north, and interior buildings were organized to a standard layout. Geographic features did occasionally affect the spacing of the forts as well as their layout; for example, Housesteads fort, near the center of the wall, was positioned to take advantage of a plentiful water supply, but the lay of the land dictated that the fort be built narrower than the others and oriented east-west instead of north-south, so it does not project north beyond the wall. The walls and buildings are constructed of local sandstone, which is plentiful along most of the wall. The encircling fort wall is 4'7 thick, thinner than Hadrian's Wall itself, but backed by an earthen rampart that all but disappeared over time.

Remains of Housesteads Fort

A view of the wall from Housesteads fort

Each fort was surrounded by at least one steep, V-shaped ditch, 18-19.5 feet wide at the top and 9-10 feet deep. After this, attackers would have to contend with a wall 4-5 feet thick and 12-14.5 feet high, and there would be a crenellated wall atop this in order to protect the defenders. The wall was also strengthened by a bank of packed turf, clay, earth, or rubble, the last generally being waste from the construction of the fort and wall itself. The banks reached all the way up to the walkway, so if there was a sudden attack a soldier could run up to the walkway from wherever he was in the fort without wasting time getting to a staircase or ladder. Towers were spaced at the corners and regular intervals along the fort's wall.

Like in forts throughout the empire, there were four gates, one for each side. The Hadrian's

Wall forts had double-portal gates topped with towers. Like the milecastles, some forts used the wall as its own north face, while others used it as the south wall and thus projected into enemy territory. While this exposed three gates to attack, apparently the Romans didn't think this was a serious risk and preferred to have the improved range of fire a projecting fort offered. Gates were placed opposite one another and connected with streets that divided the fort into four roughly equal sections.

Housesteads Fort in the central portion of the wall is one of the most excavated and best understood of the forts and thus helps scholars understand the others. The Roman name for this fort was Vercovicium, which in the local Celtic language meant "place of the effective fighters," and the fort had 10 barracks to house a cohort numbering between 800 and 1000 men. It's unclear what unit was stationed here, but by the end of the second century, it certainly was the *I Tungrorum milliaria*, "the first regiment of Tungrians a thousand strong." The Tungrians were a Germanic tribe that had crossed the Rhine and settled in what is now Belgium. Before the construction of the wall in Trajan's time, they had been stationed at Vindolanda.

An interesting detail that appears in the excavation of this and other forts is that the bread ovens were set into the bank that supported the wall. This kept them away from the interior buildings and reduced the risk of fire. Even in the cramped interior of the milecastles, the oven was set as far away from the buildings as possible.

Each fort had some buildings in common. There was the headquarters (*principia*), the garrison commander's house (*praetorium*), barracks for up to a hundred men (*centuriae*), latrines (*lavatrina*), stables (*stabuli*), workshops, (*fabricae*), and granaries (*horrea*). The headquarters was made of stone and stood along the main road (*Via Principalis*). This building was a strange combination of social and private, sacred and mundane. The front was taken up by a columned courtyard with an ambulatory around it, and beyond this stood a dais where the commander would stand and oversee important matters. Directly behind this, and giving the commander symbolic support, was a shrine (*sacellum*) that housed statues of the deified emperors, symbols of the current emperor, shrines of the main gods, and the standards for the units stationed at the fort. To either side of the shrine were offices for dealing with army bureaucracy. A locked cellar underneath the shrine housed the garrisons' treasure.

Hadrian's Wall relied on garrisons from afar, and while it may seem strange to recruit foreign soldiers to defend the empire, it was a regular part of Roman policy. By bringing potential enemies into the fold and rewarding them with money and eventual citizenship, they were neutralized and turned against more intransigent enemies. The Romans were also savvy enough to move these men far away from their native lands to fight enemies who were foreign to them. The attempt at acculturation appeared to work, since experts can identify both units from inscriptions they made on altars to Roman gods. The altar dedicated by the Tungrians is dedicated to the god Silvanus Cocidius, a blending of Roman and native British gods. Paganism was flexible in its worship, and the Romans were permissive of local gods that didn't challenge Roman supremacy. The names of the soldiers also show acculturation, with many taking Latin names while others kept their Germanic ones.

Historians now believe the forts were entirely garrisoned by auxiliary troops. The *auxilia* had all the equipment, discipline, and training of the regular legions, but with one major difference: they were not Roman citizens like the legionnaires. The *auxilia* were often recruited from subject peoples both within and outside the borders of the empire and sent to distant lands where they would have no loyalty to the local population. After 25 years' service, a soldier was given Roman citizenship, a highly valued status that was automatically given to the soldier's children.

Historians estimate around 9,000 *auxilia* manned Hadrian's Wall. There were three kinds of auxiliary units: the *alae* (cavalry), *cohortes peditatae* (infantry), and *cohortes equitatae* (mixed infantry and cavalry). Surviving records are fragmentary, but there were *alae* at three forts— Benwell, Chesters, and Stanwix—as well as at Old Carlisle and Chester-le-Street just south of the wall. Their distribution shows that they were meant to guard the two main roads leading from the wall to the north, those from Stanwix and Corbridge. Stanwix is near the western end of the wall, while Corbridge is just to the east of the central third. These cavalry units could take advantage of the roads to make swift attacks on enemy tribes.

The central portion of the wall, where the population was sparser both to the north and the south, was manned infantry. The east and the central west, which were more populated but had no main roads to the north, were manned by mixed infantry and cavalry.

Ultimately, most of Hadrian's major building programs were reserved for Rome itself. He not only built new structures but refurbished existing ones. He rebuilt the Pantheon, one of his greatest achievements, and often held court there. The project was supposed to involve a rebuilding of Agrippa's Temple, which dated back to 27 BCE, but in reality it was an entirely new structure roofed with a massive dome. It measured 142 feet across and is even larger than that of Saint Peter's Basilica. He also built his mausoleum, which today forms the base of the Pope's Castel San Angelo.

Roberta Dragan's picture of the Pantheon

Despite how impressive the other projects were, the truly outstanding architectural achievement of Hadrian's reign is thought by many to be his Villa, built near Tivoli, approximately 15 miles from Rome.

Work started on this masterpiece in 125 CE, and it was finished in 135 CE. He named different parts of the complex—stretching over 160 acres—after places he had visited. For example, one section was named the Academia in honor of Plato's school in Athens. Another was the Canopus after a sanctuary near Alexandria. He also named parts Hades and Elysium Fields. The Villa is testament to Hadrian's truly artistic talent. Within the Villa, his love of all things Greek is clear in the colonnades, statues, and porticoes. Hadrian's passion for Greece began in his boyhood when he was nicknamed "Greekling," something that remained with him throughout his life. He visited Athens on three occasions and was responsible for refurbishing many of the Greek buildings he so admired, as well as the construction of a new forum in the city he admired most.

Hadrian had an artistic temperament and was incredibly self-opinionated about the arts. He told anyone who would listen that Antimachus of Colophon was a far greater poet than Homer. Hadrian wasn't someone who brooked dissension when it came to his opinions on any matter relating to the arts, and the story of his treatment of architect Apollodorus of Damascus, a previous favorite of Trajan, does not portray him in the best of lights. Hadrian sought the architect's opinion on his design for a new temple, but the architect unwisely criticized the emperor's efforts. Apollodorus was subsequently banished, charged with what most people believe to be imaginary crimes, and put to death.[22] Others soon learned that in matters relating to the arts, it was never wise to disagree with the emperor.

Hadrian saw himself not only as a patron of the arts but as a gifted practitioner. In addition to believing that he was a skilled architect, he loved poetry and saw himself as a gifted singer and flautist. None of his literary works have survived, including his autobiography. One poem, composed on his deathbed, still exists, though the consensus is that if his other literary efforts were of a similar standard, then their loss is not a matter for much sorrow:

"O winsome wandering soul

Guest and friend of the body

To what place are you now going

Stern pale and empty?

You will be able to joke no more."[23]

Hadrian's private life has also been the subject of criticism persisting to this day. The *Historia Augusta* is highly damning in its condemnation of Hadrian's passion for young boys, but it also criticizes him for his numerous affairs with married women. He was never close to his wife, Sabina, but there is no evidence that he tried to poison her, as some have suggested. His most famous male lover was a young man named Antinous, whom Hadrian took on his travels and who met an untimely death while in Egypt. Hadrian claimed his lover had fallen off a boat while they were on the Nile, but there was speculation at the time that his death was not an accident. The story was not that Hadrian had murdered him, but that Antinous had sacrificed himself to the river for Hadrian in some arcane ritual.[24] Hadrian founded a city in his memory on the spot upon which he died, named Antinopolis.

Hadrian's grief at the death of his lover drew a certain amount of ridicule at the time, but the sniggering of the upper classes was nothing compared to the difficulties he faced in Judea. He decided to rebuild Jerusalem after it was destroyed during the Jewish Revolt in 71 BCE, and named it Aelia Capitolina. He also decided to build a new temple to Jupiter on the site of the Temple of Solomon.

Hadrian seems to have been somewhat surprised by the ferocity of the rebellion breaking out in opposition to his plans. In 132 CE, the Jews, led by Simon Bar-Kochba, were defeated by the Romans, who were eventually led by Hadrian himself. This was the only major war of Hadrian's reign, but it was incredibly costly. By the end of the rebellion in 135 CE, over 500,000 Jews had

---

[22] Cassius Dio, *Roman* History, LXIX, 4.
[23] *Historia Augusta*, Life of Hadrian, XXV, 9.
[24] *Historia Augusta*, Life of Hadrian, XIV, 5-7.

been slaughtered.

By 136 CE, Hadrian was 60 years old and in poor health. Cassius Dio wrote that he was prone to frequent nosebleeds, and various ailments led Hadrian to contemplate his mortality. He decided that the time had come to choose his successor, and he chose Lucius Ceionius Commodus, someone that everyone agreed was an excellent candidate. However, Commodus was already in the final stages of tuberculosis, and he died in early 138 CE. Hadrian did not seem too upset over the death of his heir, but he certainly wasn't pleased at the money he used to secure the people's acceptance of his nominee: "We have lost the three hundred million sesterces which we have paid out to the army and to the people, for we have leaned against a tottering wall and one which can hardly bear even our weight much less that of the empire."[25] Not only did Hadrian lose money in promoting Commodus, but he also lost considerable goodwill among the Senators after forcing two of them he suspected opposed his nomination to commit suicide.

Hadrian's overall situation in his final years was far from happy. His illness grew steadily worse, and it is now thought to have been a type of dropsy which left him incapacitated for increasingly lengthy periods. He was in such distress that at one point he asked a servant to plunge a sword into his chest, but the man, named Mastor, drew back at the final moment.

Hadrian knew that he could not continue to govern effectively, so he handed power over to Antoninus Pius, usually known as Antonine, and retired to Baiae, a famous resort favored by the Roman elite. He made his adoption of Antoninus conditional upon him naming Marcus Aurelius as his successor, and once again, the adage about the greatness of emperors being shown by the people chosen to follow proved true.

Hadrian died in Baiae in July 138 CE. His ashes were initially buried at Puteoli, near the resort, and then taken and interred in the Gardens of Domita before finally being laid to rest in his Mausoleum alongside those of his wife, who had died some years previously.

Hadrian was not popular at the time of his death. Cassius Dio wrote that he was universally hated by the people, despite the fact that Cassius Dio acknowledged his reign had, in most respects, been an excellent one. What seems to have turned the masses against him were the murders occurring at the beginning and the end of his reign. Historians have been much kinder to him, and he is often characterized as a man of liberal education who was open-minded and gave the empire stability for 20 years.

Apart from the many achievements of his reign, Hadrian is also remembered as the first emperor depicted wearing a beard. Some have suggested this was due to his love of all things Greek, but the *Historia Augusta* claimed that he wore the beard to hide skin problems, asserting, "He was tall of stature and elegant in appearance, his hair was curled on a comb and he wore a

---

[25] *Historia Augusta*, Life of Aeilus, III, 3.

full beard to cover up the natural blemishes on his face."[26]

Edward Gibbon did not doubt that Hadrian was a "good" emperor, and the famous historian described him as a benevolent dictator. He was contradictory, enigmatic, and had the capacity for both great kindness and ruthless brutality, as well as having an inordinate sense of curiosity and personal ambition. He has been compared to Mussolini and even Hitler, but Gibbon's assessment that he enabled one of the best periods in Roman history is probably a fairer judgment of him.

Antoninus Pius

An ancient statue of Antoninus Pius

Antoninus Pius was one of the most revered of the Roman emperors, even in his day, and his reputation has survived down the centuries, possibly because another great emperor, Marcus Aurelius, was so full of admiration and praise for his adopted father. Marcus Aurelius wrote, "He was always equal to the occasion, cheerful yet long sighted [sic] enough to have all his

---

[26] *Historia Augusta*, Life of Hadrian

dispositions unobtrusively perfected down to the last detail. He had an ever watchful eye to the needs of the empire, prudently conserving its resources and putting up with the criticisms that resulted. Before his gods he was not superstitious, before his fellow men he never stooped to bid for popularity or woo the masses, but pursued his own calm and steady way."[27]

Antoninus Pius was Rome's second bearded emperor, and according to contemporary sources, he was quite handsome, well-built, and physically strong. He was unusually tall for the time, and in later years his height caused him considerable difficulty, so much so that he had to wear splints of lime wood to keep his frame erect. As a result, was in a great deal of pain during his final years.

According to both contemporary accounts and modern historians, he was something of an enigma. There is a general agreement that he was a man of even temper, unambitious, and self-effacing, but he was dedicated to his role as emperor and had a strong sense of duty. He ruled for nearly 25 years, but in that time, he left much less of a mark on the empire he ruled than many who reigned for considerably shorter periods. This may be simply because his reign was one of prosperity, and he didn't want to disrupt anything. While it's fair to ask whether he simply benefitted from the hard work and success of his predecessors, he should not be underrated simply because he was not as ostentatious in his displays of power as others.

It seems likely that Hadrian chose Antoninus Pius because he considered him a safe choice, and by insisting as a condition of his adoption that Antoninus adopt Marcus Aurelius as his successor, Hadrian ensured Rome would be in capable hands for some time. If, as some suggest, Hadrian saw Antoninus as someone to hold the reins until the talented Marcus Aurelius reached maturity, then he certainly chose well. At the time of his adoption, Antoninus had no living sons, and at the age of 51, he was unlikely to sire any others. In due course, his daughter, Faustina, married Marcus Aurelius, but it's unlikely that Hadrian had considered the possibility that Antoninus Pius would live to the exceptionally old age of 74 and reign longer than any emperor since Augustus.

Titus Aurelius Fulvus Boionus Arrius Antoninus was born in September 86 CE at Lanuvium, 20 miles south of Rome. His family had come from around Nemausus in Gaul and had been successful in climbing the Roman social ladder. His grandfather had been a Consul on two occasions, and his father, Titus, was Consul in 89 CE.

As a boy, Antoninus was brought up on his family's estate in Etruria. He built himself a palace there, where he spent much of his time as emperor. His father died when he was young, so he was raised by his paternal grandfather, and then by his maternal grandfather. They were both extremely wealthy, and Antoninus inherited plenty. He rose through the ranks until he became Consul in 120 CE and Governor of Asia in 135 CE.

---

[27] Marcus Aurelius, *Meditations*, I.16.

Despite these posts, his overall administrative experience was quite limited in comparison to many of his class, and, unlike the vast majority of his peers, he had no military experience. The year he spent as a governor is the only known time that he ventured outside of Italy. His lack of interest in travel stands in marked contrast to Hadrian's constant journeying.

Antoninus was adopted by Hadrian in 138 CE, less than six months before the latter's death. The transfer of power was peaceful, and Antoninus seemed disinclined to do anything that might rock the boat. Many officials appointed by Hadrian were left in post, and Antoninus' demeanour soon won the Senate's favor. At the time, Fronto wrote of him, "Antoninus I love, I cherish like the light, like day, like breath and feel that I am loved by him." Even allowing for the rather hyperbolic sycophancy, similar praise from other sources confirm he was already admired at the start of his reign.

There was one point of major contention between the new emperor and the Senate in relation to Hadrian's divine honors. The Senate dug its heels in and refused to deify Antoninus' predecessor, but the emperor was also stubborn and threatened not to govern if Hadrian was not deified. He won the battle of wills, and Hadrian was duly raised to the status of a god. Whether Antoninus took the Senate on out of his affection, respect, and love for Hadrian, or because he felt that a refusal to honor his adoptive father was a slight on himself that would weaken his prestige, is unknown. Though he authorized repairs to existing buildings and monuments during his reign, most notably the Colloseum, Antoninus was responsible for only two new buildings in Rome: one temple dedicated to Hadrian and the other to himself and his wife, Faustina.

The Temple of Antoninus and Faustina

Antoninus was surprisingly disinterested when it came to involving himself in military matters, especially for a Roman aristocrat and ruler. At the same time, he was prepared to spend time on the minute details of government, which was also unusual for a nobleman. He introduced new laws regulating the treatment of slaves, making it illegal to sexually abuse or subject them to excessive cruelty. There were only two instances of treason against him during his reign, and the conspirators were given proper trials. Unlike what had happened in similar situations under previous emperors, he did not pursue their friends and families in the hope of discovering further traitors. Consent, not coercion, appears to have been the normal mode of operation in Antoninus' approach to rule.

Considering his wealth, he was not prone to self-indulgent or extravagant displays, indicating that he deserved the name of Pius ("Respectful") that had been bestowed upon him by the Senate. The *Historia Augusta* gives a detailed explanation as to why he was awarded this name: "He was given the name Pius by the Senate, either because he supported his frail and elderly father in law [sic] with his arm when he was attending the Senate, or because he reprieved those whom Hadrian in ill health had ordered killed, or because he decreed great and limitless honours to Hadrian after his death against the general will or because when Hadrian wished to kill himself he prevented him from doing so by great care and diligence, or because he was truly a most compassionate man by nature and did nothing severe in his time."[28]

Antoninus ruled the empire either from Rome or his nearby palace at Lorium, never venturing far from the city. The *Historia Augusta* suggests that he adopted this policy for two reasons: "He did not travel on any expeditions except to visit his own estates for he said the retinue of even a frugal prince was a great weight for provincials to bear. And yet he was considered a man of great authority by all peoples for residing in the city so that in this central location he could receive messengers quickly wherever they came from."[29]

Though he was more than happy to stay at home, he chose and utilized able governors and generals, which allowed for order and prosperity throughout the empire. While there was no major war during his 23 years as emperor, he did have to deal with unrest that could have escalated into more serious conflagrations had they not been dealt with in a timely manner.

One specific venture he did authorize, which was about extending the empire, was the expedition into Scotland. The *Historia Augusta* recorded, "He defeated the Britons through his governor Lollius Urbicus and having driven off the barbarians built a second wall of turf."[30]

Unlike Hadrian, Antoninus directed his campaign in Britain through Lollius but was still acclaimed imperator after "his success." He ordered Hadrian's Wall to be abandoned and built a new one, half the length between the Rivers Forth and Clyde, with the intention of incorporating all of southern Scotland into the empire, but even before his death, he ordered the Romans to reinstate the boundary back at Hadrian's Wall.

From the safety of Rome, Antoninus successfully managed to quell rebellions in Mauretania, Germany, Egypt, Judea, and Greece, as well as deal with threats from Dacia and Parthia. It is to his credit that he managed to negotiate peaceful resolutions to a number of these disturbances.

During his reign, Rome celebrated its 900th anniversary in 148 CE, an event that occasioned massive celebrations and an outpouring of goodwill toward Antoninus. He died after a short illness in March 161 CE, and it is said that his last action as emperor was to give the password of the day to the duty officer before he died, choosing "equanimity" as the final password.

He was immediately deified by the Senate and his remains taken to the Mausoleum of Hadrian. This burial was one of Antoninus' few innovations, for unlike his predecessors, he was not cremated but interred, setting a new fashion followed by subsequent emperors. His biographer wrote of him, "Almost alone of all emperors he lived entirely unsullied by the blood of either

---

[28] *Historia Augusta*, Life of Antoninus Pius, II, 3.
[29] *Historia Augusta,* Life of Antoninus Pius, VII, 11.
[30] *Historia Augusta*, Life of Antoninus Pius, V, 4.

citizen or foe so far as was in his power, and he was justly compared to Numa whose good fortune and tranquillity and religious rites he ever maintained."

Historian J.B. Bury wrote that "however estimable the man, Antoninus was hardly a great statesman. The rest which the Empire enjoyed under his auspices had been rendered possible through Hadrian's activity, and was not due to his own exertions; on the other hand, he carried the policy of peace at any price too far, and so entailed calamities on the state after his death. He not only had no originality or power of initiative, but he had not even the insight or boldness to work further on the new lines marked out by Hadrian." Still, the consensus is that Antoninus was one of the most capable rulers Rome ever had. He is credited with restoring the status of the Senate. While some have characterized him as plodding and patient, it is clear that he was a born administrator. He restored some of the Senate's former glory without relinquishing imperial power, and he used that power to strengthen the empire in unexciting and mundane ways. He improved and repaired buildings rather than construct new ones, and his principal contribution to the empire was the development of an efficient system of governance. His particular weakness lay in his lack of military acumen, which meant he did not put as much effort into the improvement of the Roman military, but by choosing Antoninus' successor ahead of time, Hadrian ensured the next emperor would have the ability to deal with the external threats that began to pose real problems for the empire's security.

Jean-Pol Grandmont's picture of an ancient statue of Antoninus in military garb

Marcus Aurelius

Eric Gaba's picture of a bust of Marcus Aurelius

Marcus Aurelius was born into a wealthy, politically active family in Rome in April 121 CE. His grandfather, Annius Verus, was a Consul on three occasions, while his mother, Domitia Lucilla, was wealthy in her own right. His father, also named Annius Verus, died when he was very young, so his education was overseen by his grandfather. It was at the tender age of 6 that he was enrolled in the Equestrian Order, and two years later he became a Salian priest.

It was not long before the young Marcus Aurelius came to the attention of Hadrian, who called him Verissimus "Truthful") and oversaw much of the youngster's upbringing from that point forward. Hadrian ensured that he had the best tutors available, one of whom was historian Cornelius Fronto, and it is obvious that Hadrian had marked Marcus out for advancement to the highest levels from a very early age.

When he nominated Lucius Aelius as his first successor, Hadrian arranged a marriage between his daughter and his protégé, and when Aelius died suddenly, Hadrian chose Antoninus Pius as his successor on the condition that he adopt Marcus Aurelius into his family along with Lucius Verus, the son of the deceased Aelius. Thus, when Antoninus succeeded Hadrian, it was clear to all that Marcus Aurelius was the designated heir. To that end, Marcus Aurelius divorced Aelius's daughter and married Faustina the Younger, daughter of Antoninus.

An ancient bust of Faustina the Younger

A depiction of Marcus Aurelius and Lucius Verus

The next several years were nothing less than an apprenticeship in the art of ruling. He held the position of Consul in 140 CE, 145 CE, and again in 146 CE, as well as numerous others in the intervening years. By the time Antoninus died, Marcus Aurelius was well-educated in the business of governing, but he decided that the task of ruling the vast Roman Empire was too great for one man and asked that Lucius Verus be raised to imperial status upon his succession. The *Historia Augusta* noted, "Being forced by the Senate to assume the government of the state after the death of the Deified Pius, Marcus made his brother his colleague in the empire, giving him the name Lucius Aurelius Verus Commodus and bestowing on him the titles Caesar and Augustus. They began to rule the state on equal terms and then it was that the Roman Empire first had two Emperors when he shared with another the empire left to him."[31]

Despite the fact that Marcus Aurelius was the more experienced and talented of the two, they worked well together until Lucius Verus died eight years later, leaving Marcus Aurelius as the sole ruler. Though its debut was short-lived, the practice of sharing power became a regular feature of imperial government in the later years of the empire.

While external threats were minimal during Antoninus Pius' reign, they had nevertheless grown, the very reason some historians criticized him for being too timid. Marcus had to face major threats, making his reign one of constant defense of the empire's boundaries. In the east, the Parthians invaded Armenia under Vologases III and inflicted two major defeats on Roman

---

[31] *Historia Augusta*, Life of Marcus Aurelius, VII.

armies sent to deal with the incursion. Marcus Aurelius sent Lucius Verus as the head of a much larger force, and by 166 CE, the Romans had expelled the Parthians and Lucius Verus returned to Rome in triumph.

Unfortunately for the Romans, that success brought a major disaster in the form of plague throughout the empire. It is now believed that the plague spread as a result of the troops' return from the front. Some estimates put the number of deaths in the millions, and during the epidemic, Marcus Aurelius brought Galen, the famous medical expert, to Italy to advise on how to cope with the illness.

Along with the plague, trouble erupted in the west. In 166 CE, tribes on the Danube frontier found themselves under severe pressure from tribes migrating from the east, and they began to force their way across the border. This was the start of what became known as the Marcomannic Wars, which lasted for the rest of Marcus Aurelius' life. Italy itself was threatened by the movements of tribes, such as the Marcomanni and the Langobardi, but they were only two tribes among many determined to settle in Roman territory.

The co-emperors shared command of the legions, countering the influx of tribesmen from the east, but Lucius died in 169 CE. Marcus Aurelius' co-emperor received mixed press from Roman historians. Compared to Marcus Aurelius himself, his abilities and successes have been judged as negligible. The *Historia Augusta* is far from complimentary, describing Lucius as vain, idle, and interested only in his own pleasure: "Verrus took such pride in his yellow hair that he used to sift gold dust on his head in order that his hair thus brightened, might seem yellower."[32] At the same time, the *Historia* also noted "that he should not be classed with either the good or the bad Emperors since it is agreed that while he did not bristle with vices no more did he abound in virtues."[33] The writers concluded that he was a bit silly, but not really vicious or harmful.

---

[32] *Historia Augusta*, Life of Verrus, X.6.
[33] *Historia Augusta*, Life of Verrus, X.6.

An ancient bust of Lucius Verus

The truth probably lies in another statement. The work noted that Lucius Verus "obeyed Marcus Aurelius whenever he entered upon any undertaking as a lieutenant obeys a proconsul or a governor obeys the emperor."[34] In *Meditations*, Marcus Aurelius summed up his co-emperor as follows: "A brother whose natural qualities were a standing challenge to my own self-discipline at the same time as his deferential affection warmed my heart."[35] It seems that Lucius may have lacked natural abilities, but he could be relied upon to act as a good second-in-command, and Marcus Aurelius benefitted from this characteristic during an extremely fraught period. Upon Lucius' death, Marcus Aurelius had to confront issues facing the empire by himself. Whether Lucius had been of any significant help to him is a bit of a moot point given that the emperor missed him on a personal level, and perhaps also as an aide.

Marcus Aurelius devised a plan to end the problem by invading the territories of the migrating tribes, strengthening Rome's imperial defenses at the same time. By 175 CE, he had stemmed the

---

[34] *Historia Augusta*, Life of Verrus, X.5.
[35] Marcus Aurelius, *Meditations*

flow of tribesmen into Roman lands and subsequently made plans to take the fight to the tribesmen's homelands.

Eventually, these plans were cut short by the revolt of Avidius Cassius, who had been set up as king by Marcus Aurelius in Armenia years earlier. A rumor circulated in Armenia that Marcus Aurelius had been killed on the Danube, and Cassius took the opportunity to declare himself emperor. Marcus Aurelius returned to Rome, and the attempted coup collapsed.

Marcus Aurelius then set out for the east, but it was on that journey that his wife, Faustina the Younger, died. The empress gave birth to 14 children, 6 of whom survived into adulthood, but in her later years, she was renowned for her succession of lovers, many of whom she manipulated Marcus Aurelius into giving positions throughout the empire. This indulgence of his wife's infidelities and his apparent willingness to promote her lovers did not go down well with Roman society and is one of the few blemishes on his career. Despite the rumors of her trysts with gladiators and sailors, Marcus Aurelius loved her deeply, and when she died, he ensured that she was deified. He never remarried, though he did take a concubine.

The emperor returned to Rome in 176 CE, planning once again to end the ongoing problems along the Danube frontier. He took his son, Commodus, with him on this campaign, and by 179 CE, the Marcomanni had been crushed to the point that they were virtually extinct. He intended to carry out what today would be called ethnic cleansing so that the area east of the Danube could be settled and become a Roman province. Trajan, too, had dreamed of creating a new province in the region, and like him, Marcus Aurelius would not succeed. In 180 CE, Marcus Aurelius fell ill and handed power over to his son before dying shortly thereafter.

Those campaigns were not the only difficulties Marcus Aurelius had to face during his reign. The wars were ruinously expensive, and the sound financial practices of his predecessors, though enabling him to finance the conflicts, did not provide a bottomless money pit. Revenues dropped, and in 169 CE, Marcus Aurelius resorted to auctioning imperial property off to pay his troops. Desperate for money, he took more and more control away from local administrators, thus consolidating and increasing the degree of centralization initiated by his predecessors.

The financial concerns also meant that unlike his immediate predecessors, Marcus Aurelius was never in a position to embark on major building projects. The two best known projects are both memorials to his campaigns: the Aurelian Column and a triumphal arch. The column was 100 Roman feet in height, contained a spiraling relief depicting events during his Danube campaigns. It was quite obviously modeled on Trajan's Column, a gift from the Senate that stood outside the temple dedicated to him. The arch has completely disappeared, though some of the panels decorating it were re-used on the Arch of Constantine.

There are very few physical remains that demonstrate Marcus Aurelius' impact on Rome and his legacy. One of the reasons Marcus Aurelius is considered a truly great emperor is due to writings of his that survived. He was a Stoic, and much of his philosophy was passed down in a 12-book record of his reflections, confessions, and warnings. The books were entitled *To Myself*, but they are now known as the *Meditations*. They were written in the later years of his life while on campaign on the Danube. It has been suggested that he wrote them to console himself during the long years of privation he endured while prosecuting the war.

His core belief was in the principle of virtue through duty to oneself and others. Much of his writing is quite dark, and he repeatedly reflects on the nearness of death and the transitory nature of human existence.

His thoughts, on the other hand, confirm that he was a genuine thinker and a true philosopher king. He wrote, "The first rule is to keep an untroubled spirit, for all things must bow to Nature's law and soon enough you must vanish into nothingness, like Hadrian and Augustus. The second is to look things in the face and know them for what they are remembering that it is your duty to be a good man. Do without flinching what man's nature demands, say what seems to you most just though with courtesy modesty and sincerity."[36]

The *Historia Augusta* described Marcus Aurelius as "a solemn child from the very beginning and as soon as he passed beyond the age when children are brought up under the care of nurses, he was handed over to advanced instructors and attained to a knowledge of philosophy… He studied philosophy with ardour even as a youth. For when he was twelve years old he adopted the dress and a little later the hardiness of a philosopher, pursuing his studies clad in a rough Greek cloak and sleeping on the ground. [A]t his mother's solicitation however, he reluctantly consented to sleep on a couch strewn with skins.[37]

On the basis of this information, it does not seem likely that he enjoyed a fun and frivolous childhood, and his upbringing undoubtedly shaped his later life, especially his fascination with philosophy. Clearly, that philosophy proved so important in shaping his decisions.

---

[36] Marcus Aurelius, *Meditations,* VIII.5.
[37] *Historia Augusta*, Life of Marcus II.1.

A bust of Marcus Aurelius as a young boy

Marcus Aurelius was not the most optimistic of men. Some might say he was simply pragmatic and honest about life, but his attitude was certainly quite depressing. In *Meditations*, he wrote, "Consider for the sake of argument the times of Vespasian. You will see all the same things, men marrying, begetting children, being ill, dying, fighting wars, feasting, trading, farming, flattering, asserting themselves, suspecting, praying for the death of others, grumbling at their present lot, coveting a consulate, coveting a kingdom. Then turn to the times of Trajan, again everything is the same and that life too is dead."[38]

Despite his pessimism, it can be said that, on a personal level, Marcus Aurelius was a good man who defended the territory of the empire in an exemplary fashion. However, if one of the

---

[38] Marcus Aurelius, *Meditations,* IV.32.

main criteria used to determine the success of an emperor is the successor he chooses, then Marcus Aurelius failed spectacularly. He was the first emperor since Vespasian, who had ruled about 100 years before, to leave his son as his successor, and the alacrity with which Marcus Aurelius abandoned the principle of adoption suggests that traditional family ties would have exerted an influence on the choice of emperor sooner if his predecessors had sons to whom the throne could be passed.

Commodus stands alongside Caligula as one of the Roman emperors who contemporaries considered absolutely vile. Commodus became notorious for his paranoia, murdering anyone he suspected of conspiracy and ruling like an absolute dictator way out of his depth. While Marcus Aurelius struggled with depleted funds, Commodus used them to pay his own appearance fees as a gladiator, during which he won fixed matches against real gladiators or beat to death physically disabled individuals and amputees who had been rounded up and tethered together for the spectacle. Commodus also killed all kinds of animals in the arena, and on one occasion beheaded an ostrich and carried it over to the gallery holding various Roman Senators, implicitly threatening to do the same to them.

In the final years, Commodus took things to new heights by renaming the city of Rome to *Colonia Lucia Annia Commodiana*, renaming the months of the year after himself, and depicting himself as a god of herculean strength. The zaniness ended with the assassination of Commodus in 192, which spelled the end of the Nerva–Antonine dynasty and led to civil wars that made 193 the "Year of the Five Emperors," much the same way Nero's death touched off the "Year of the Four Emperors" over 100 years earlier.

Cassius Dio wrote that Commodus was "not naturally wicked but, on the contrary, as guileless as any man that ever lived. His great simplicity, however, together with his cowardice, made him the slave of his companions, and it was through them that he at first, out of ignorance, missed the better life and then was led on into lustful and cruel habits, which soon became second nature."

A bust depicting Commodus as Hercules

In general, despite the one very glaring failure that Commodus represented, Marcus Aurelius ruled with scrupulous care. He was a rigid conservative, especially when it came to maintaining the existing social order, but he was lenient in his rulings and displayed a humanity nearly above reproach. He has often been described as cold and joyless, but his overriding motivation was duty, and in the performance of his duty as he viewed it, he excelled.

Conclusion

The reigns of the Five Good Emperors were undoubtedly the high point of the Roman Empire, which its greatest extent territorially and enjoyed a degree of prosperity and (relative) political tranquility unmatched in any other period of similar length. The fact that they all played their parts in reforms, rebuilt and carried out new construction, and promoted policies which saw the further integration and Romanization of the numerous races within the empire's boundaries is to their collective credit. The five rulers had very different personalities, and it can be argued that the complementary nature of their skills played a part in maintaining this prolonged period of success. Another factor was that they were all chosen to succeed to the throne, rather than having inherited it by dint of direct descent from the previous emperor or seizing power through brute force or subterfuge. This gave them a legitimacy that, when coupled with their natural talents, enabled them to make their own contributions to the empire, and significant ones at that.

Whether the use of the term "good" is appropriate in the characterization of these individuals matters far less than the fact that each ruled in a way that resulted in a positive outcome for the empire. The one negative aspect of their reigns stems from their authoritarian, centralizing tendencies, because no matter how well-intentioned or effective that form of government was in their hands, it paved the way for future problems. That greater degree of centralization worked well in the hands of someone like Marcus Aurelius, but it was utterly disastrous just a few years later when wielded by Commodus.

In the 19th century, Matthew Arnold concluded that the Five Good Emperors "lived and acted in a state of society modern by its essential characteristics, in an epoch akin to our own in a brilliant centre of civilisation."[39] Even though modern historians are now more aware of the inherent weaknesses in the Roman Empire at this time, it is still fair to conclude that these five emperors deserve the epithet that has marked their legacies for centuries.

Online Resources

Other books about Rome by Charles River Editors

Other books about ancient history by Charles River Editors

Other books about the Five Good Emperors on Amazon

Further Reading

Ackermann, Marsha E.; Schroeder, Michael J.; Terry, Jancie J.; Lo Upshur, Jiu-Hwa; Whitters, Mark F. Encyclopedia of World History, Ackerman-Schroeder-Terry-Hwa Lo, 2008: Encyclopedia of World History. New York: Facts on File, 2008.

Adams, Geoff W. Marcus Aurelius in the Historia Augusta and Beyond. Lanham, MD: Lexington Books, 2013. ISBN 9780739176382.

An, Jiayao. "When Glass Was Treasured in China". Annette L. Juliano and Judith A. Lerner (eds), Nomads, Traders, and Holy Men Along China's Silk Road, 79–94. Turnhout, Belgium: Brepols Publishers, 2002. ISBN 9782503521787.

Astarita, Maria L. Avidio Cassio (in Italian). Rome: Edizione di Storia e Letteratura, 1983.

---

[39] M. Arnold, *The Victoria Magazine* 2 (1863).

Ball, Warwick. Rome in the East: Transformation of an Empire, 2nd edition. London: Routledge, 2016. ISBN 9780415720786.

Barnes, Timothy D. "Hadrian and Lucius Verus". Journal of Roman Studies 57:1–2 (1967): 65–79. doi:10.2307/299345. JSTOR 299345.

Barnes, Timothy D. "Legislation Against the Christians". Journal of Roman Studies, Vol. 58 (1968): 32–50. doi:10.2307/299693. JSTOR 299693.

Barnes, Timothy D. "Some Persons in the Historia Augusta", Phoenix 26:2 (1972): 140–182. doi:10.2307/1087714. JSTOR 1087714.

Beard, Mary. "Was He Quite Ordinary?". London Review of Books 31:14, 23 July 2009.

Beckmann, Martin. Column of Marcus Aurelius. Oxford Classical Dictionary, 2015. doi:10.1093/acrefore/9780199381135.013.8058.

Benario, Herbert W. "Marcus Aurelius (A.D. 161-180)". Roman Emperors.

Birley, Anthony R. Marcus Aurelius: A Biography. London: Routledge, 1966, rev. 1987. ISBN 9781134695690.

Birley, Anthony R. "Hadrian to the Antonines". In The Cambridge Ancient History Volume XI: The High Empire, A.D. 70–192, edited by Alan Bowman, Peter Garnsey, and Dominic Rathbone, 132–94. Cambridge: Cambridge University Press, 2000. ISBN 9780521263351.

Bowman, John L. A Reference Guide to Stoicism. Bloomington, IN: Author House, 2014. ISBN 9781496900173.

Bury, John Bagnell. The Student's Roman Empire: A History of the Roman Empire from Its Foundation to the Death of Marcus Aurelius (27 B. C.--180 A. D.). New York: Harper, 1893.

Champlin, Edward. "The Chronology of Fronto". Journal of Roman Studies 64 (1974): 136–59. doi:10.2307/299265. JSTOR 299265.

Champlin, Edward. Fronto and Antonine Rome. Cambridge, MA: Harvard University Press, 1980. ISBN 9780674331778.

Collins, Desmond. Background to Archaeology: Britain in Its European Setting. Cambridge: Cambridge University Press Archive, 1973. GGKEY:XUFU58U7ESS.

De Crespigny, Rafe. A Biographical Dictionary of Later Han to the Three Kingdoms (23–220 AD). Boston: Brill, 2007. ISBN 9789047411840.

Duncan-Jones, Richard. Structure and Scale in the Roman Economy. Cambridge: Cambridge University Press, 1990. ISBN 9780521892896.

Equestrian Statue of Marcus Aurelius. Musei Capitolini.

Gagarin, Michael. The Oxford Encyclopedia of Ancient Greece and Rome, Volume 7. Oxford: Oxford University Press, 2010. ISBN 9780195170726.

Gibbon, Edward. History of the Decline and Fall of the Roman Empire – Volume 2.

Gilliam, J. F. "The Plague under Marcus Aurelius". American Journal of Philology 82.3 (1961): 225–251. doi:10.2307/292367. JSTOR 292367.

Grant, Michael. The Antonines: The Roman Empire in Transition. London: Routledge, 2016. ISBN 9781317972105.

Francesco Gnecchi, I medaglioni Romani, 3 Vols, Milan, 1912.

Grant, Michael. The Climax Of Rome. London: Orion, 2011. ISBN 9781780222769.

Furtak, Rick Anthony. "Marcus Aurelius: Kierkegaard's Use and Abuse of the Stoic Emperor". In Kierkegaard and the Roman World, edited by Jon Stewart, 69–74. Farnham, England: Ashgate Publishing, 2009. ISBN 9780754665540.

Hadot, Pierre. The Inner Citadel: The Meditations of Marcus Aurelius. Cambridge, MA: Harvard University Press, 1998. ISBN 9780674461710.

Haeser, Heinrich. Lehrbuch der Geschichte der Medicin und der epidemischen Krankenheiten III. 1875.

Hays, Gregory. Meditations. London: Weidenfeld & Nicolson, 2003. ISBN 9781842126752.

Kemezis, Adam M. Greek Narratives of the Roman Empire under the Severans: Cassius Dio, Philostratus and Herodian. Cambridge University Press, 2014. ISBN 9781107062726.

Kleiner, Fred S. Gardner's Art Throughout the Ages: the Western Perspective. Mason, OH: Cengage Learning, 2008. ISBN 9780495573555.

Le Bohec, Yann. The Imperial Roman Army. Routledge, 2013. ISBN 9781135955137.

Lendering, Jona. "Antoninus and Aelius". Livius.org.

Lendering, Jona. "Lucilla". Livius.org.

Lendering, Jona. "Marcus Aurelius". Livius.org.

Levick, Barbara M. Faustina I and II: Imperial Women of the Golden Age. New York: Oxford University Press, 2014. ISBN 9780199702176.

Mattingly, Harold; Sydenham, Edward A. The Roman Imperial Coinage, vol. III, Antoninus Pius to Commodus. London: Spink & Son, 1930.

Mark, Joshua. "Marcus Aurelius: Plato's Philosopher King". Ancient History Encyclopedia. 8 May 2018.

Mellor, Ronald, review of Edward Champlin's Fronto and Antonine Rome, American Journal of Philology 103:4 (1982).

Merrony, Mark. The Plight of Rome in the Fifth Century AD. London: Routledge, 2017. ISBN 9781351702782.

Millar, Fergus. The Roman Near East: 31 BC – AD 337. Cambridge, MA: Harvard University Press, 1993. ISBN 9780674778863.

McLynn, Frank. Marcus Aurelius: A Life. New York: Da Capo Press, 2009. ISBN 9780306819162.

McLynn, Frank. Marcus Aurelius: Warrior, Philosopher, Emperor. London: Bodley Head, 2009. ISBN 9780224072922. Online review.

Murphy, Verity. "Past pandemics that ravaged Europe". BBC News, 7 November 2005.

Plague in the Ancient World. http://people.loyno.edu.

Portrait of the Emperor Marcus Aurelius. The Walters Art Museum.

Pulleyblank, Edwin G.; Leslie, D. D.; Gardiner, K. H. J. "The Roman Empire as Known to Han China". Journal of the American Oriental Society, 1999. 119 (1). doi:10.2307/605541. JSTOR 605541.

Reed, J. Eugene. The Lives of the Roman Emperors and Their Associates from Julius Cæsar (B. C. 100) to Agustulus (A. D. 476). Philadelphia, PA: Gebbie & Company, 1883.

"Roman Currency of the Principate". Tulane.edu. Archived 10 February 2001.

Stephens, William O. Marcus Aurelius: A Guide for the Perplexed. London: Continuum, 2012. ISBN 9781441125613.

Stertz, Stephen A. "Marcus Aurelius as Ideal Emperor in Late-Antique Greek Thought". The Classical World 70:7 (1977): 433–39. doi:10.2307/4348712. JSTOR 4348712.

Syme, Ronald. "The Ummidii". Historia 17:1 (1968): 72–105. JSTOR 4435015.

Thinkers at War. Military History Monthly, published August 2014. This is the conclusion of Ian King's biography of Marcus Aurelius.

Van Ackeren, Marcel. A Companion to Marcus Aurelius. New York: Wiley, 2012. ISBN 9781118219829.

Weigel, Richard D. "Antoninus Pius (A.D. 138–161)". Roman Emperors.

Young, Gary K. Rome's Eastern Trade: International Commerce and Imperial Policy, 31 BC – AD 305. London: Routledge, 2001. ISBN 9781134547937.

Free Books by Charles River Editors

We have brand new titles available for free most days of the week. To see which of our titles are currently free, click on this link.

Discounted Books by Charles River Editors

We have titles at a discount price of just 99 cents everyday. To see which of our titles are currently 99 cents, click on this link.

Printed in Great Britain
by Amazon

49682197R00032